the day is
ready for you

also by alison malee
shifting bone

the day is
ready for you

alison malee

Andrews McMeel
PUBLISHING®

be brave. the day is ready for you.

this book is a small bird fluttering outside a window. i want you, dear reader, to be the hand. the opened latch. the wide eyes. the *please, stay awhile.*

for the wild dreamer,

let these words sneak up behind you.
let them tap you on the shoulder.
let it be the most unexpected surprise.

for the lost and stumbling,

let these words be the language
you needed to breathe again.

for the little girl i once was,

let these words make you proud.
let this honesty be a sign of forgiveness.

for you,
i have saved all of these moments.

some sway like untouched ghosts,
some roar and spit and rattle.

some, drifting lilies.
some, like clay in the wet, wet burrows of earth.

for the family i never knew,

i want you to know about
the things that have happened.
the people i have been along the way.
the world as i have come to know it.

for the people who
have always held my manic heart,

i hope you understand.

contents

unmovable
things

the day is ready for you

never

nothing about love is easy.
we are always too loud,
sometimes too soft.
always too caged,
sometimes too free.

no one ever told me
that love *is the teeth*
that bite your lip
without apology.

the blood that runs.

the first aid kit.
the alcohol, the gauze,
the sting.

the mouth that
kisses, k i s s e s, kisses
it better.

or the mouth that tells you
there was never
any wound at all.

will be

in this way, the undertow
is only a metaphor for surviving.
do you understand?
the currents only exist to explain grief.

so when i tell you i am drowning,
i mean that, today,
the loss sits on my chest
less like a paperweight
and more like air turned
carbon monoxide without warning.

the earth spins consistently.

most days i am ready for it.
and when i can breathe, i am floating.
the ocean swallow is a sometimes. you know?
it moves quickly.

but see the sun through the rippling water,
the light, it is close. do you understand?
do you understand now?

i am telling you i have been injured
by an unknown thing.
injured but not conquered.
i kick. i fling arms through salt and crash.
i fight my way to the surface.

in this way, though i am not now,
i will be fine.

the day is ready for you

both of us

this heart and i
spend all day
wanting.

(it eats us up like wildfire.)

alone

i look for you between time-thickened shadows,
in the one open window. beneath moth-bitten lace.
at the outskirts of town. in the deep end of the
     public pool.
at the country club somewhere in the midst
of dollar signs and tightened skin.

i empty the ocean. peel sand from the fins of every
     beast.
i try to gargle salt for you just
to see if you exist between molecules.

but you do not raise your hand or speak
or pull yourself from the inside of a thrift store
     baseball cap.

so i write you instead.
i write you into morning eyes, sleep hazy in the
     corners.
into froth and sip and burnt tongues.
into honey-coated berries, ripe from nothing.

into some meadow, high and above it all.
flowers pungent as they weave between breaths,
breaths humid and silent as they
brush against wax petals.

most days i write you into things that disappear.
sometimes i write you into concrete.

i am either not alone or impossibly. nothing lingers.

the day is ready for you

<u>right</u>

good, they say. *good,* who deserves love, really?
why should anyone be loved, really?
isn't it better if love sugars only the hands of a few,
    anyway?
not you, anyway. never you, anyway.

and maybe i am just as rage driven and envious.
maybe i do put my hands on the wheel only to crash.
because when you leave, all reason leaves with you.

suddenly i am aching teeth and blackberry limbs,
    only.
i inhale. inhale. face bloodred and salted.
scream, *take me with you.*
and it is so big in such an empty space. it echoes on.

i think i hear the walls whisper,
they were right. they were right. they were right.
and the floors groan and laugh with them.
but the windows stay closed. the doors stay closed.
still, i am a puddle. waiting.

maybe they were right. maybe love is an escape
    room.
maybe i am the thing that needs escaping.

it is a growling tickle in my stomach.
this knowledge, this coaxed truth:
it did not stay like i thought it would.

not for me, anyway. never for me, anyway.

citrus

anger makes it easier to say
the lemon words,
the swollen sentences.

makes it easier to throw punches
without the memory of bruised skin.

you lick your lips and i
come away infuriated.

we will wake up tomorrow
sore and sour.
but i will empty the whole
ice tray into my water glass
before you make it
to the kitchen.

and i will leave lemon slices,
tart and lonely,
around the house.

and i will let
your cheek blister purple
before i ever admit
to the taste of citrus.

the day is ready for you

mountains

big, unmovable things:
like mountains,
like desire.

stand still

your voice leaves me quiet.

it echoes. (again and again.)

i want to tell you *settle down*.
i want to tell you there is no need
for all this loud.

forget your restlessness.

but i say nothing.
so the cobwebs
stretch and weave
with vigor.

the muscles stop
their clench and unravel.

my throat grows
blue-black icicle veins.

my throat becomes its own island.
my throat does not flag down
the rescue team.

my throat sees help and
stands still.

every time.

the day is ready for you

strange thing

this heart is deeply, deeply hidden.
like an old wooden box under the bed
stuffed with secrets.

mostly, love notes. though also, postcards.
handprints. glimpses. people who don't belong
anymore but are. just are, still.

and i find it like i find the universe at dawn. quietly.
like it is still groggy from all the dark hours.
hungover from sleep.
i sneak up carefully and try to pick the lock.
it bites at my wrists. chews. spits in my eye.

it is a strange thing.
a fickle thing.

yet i come again. try again. bring better keys.
sometimes it opens. sometimes i stand around
    waiting.

sometimes i am missing fingers before breakfast.

it is a strange, strange thing.
a good thing.

vicious but mine.

in the air

i am reckless.
i go out in spaghetti straps
and pretend winter arrived
only yesterday.
or i see my breath dancing
outside my body frantically.
have a good laugh
at my own expense,
and throw my bird arms up
like wings for good measure.
i let the frost eat at my sandals,
readjust my skirt till it
sits above my knees.
and when they ask about the cold,
i will tell them, like i've told you,
i am gasoline.
i am, more than i am not,
fire fuel skin.
i am burning.
but i swear,
it is just
something
in the air.

the day is ready for you

obvious

what could i say? i tend to lean more toward
roses than bloodied palms, but okay. i say, *okay*.
(still, it seems like too much, too obvious somehow.)

i take all of the ache and hold it in my arms like
    sandpaper.
i smile until my bottom lip splits right open.
the skin on my hands scratch, scratches
away over time but still i hold on.

no one explains grief like this.
how you can be here in one moment.
and then crushed beneath an enveloping roar
at the back of your throat.

how it is, at first, so quiet you do not even notice it is
    there.
how it wakes you up in whispered (screaming)
    heartbeats.
how after it becomes less of a tolerable tickle
and more of a bloodthirst there is no immediate cure.

once, i spent a whole day holding my breath.
i thought it would cling to my ribs like muscle.
but it was too free to linger, and my nose let it all
    escape silently.
i admit, some days i must do this.

because 1.) am i still living? and 2.) how can i exist in
    such a way
that i never have to question this again? you know?
i don't have the answer yet.

see, what do you say when someone gifts you agony?
i say, *okay. okay.*
(i do not want it. take it back. take it back.)

but, okay. i say, *okay.*

and somehow it still seems too obvious.

the day is ready for you

does it

i don't know how to close a door
without the windows shattering, too.
this heart is slam and stomp and rage.

once, a lady before me in a checkout line
told her son that it was time to leave. he tossed his
    head angrily in answer.
avoided her eyes. dragged his feet along the tile.

i wanted to laugh but i knew. i throw the same fit.
    every time.
only i yell louder. drag my feet harder.

the woman does not even bat an eye, says,
everything comes to an end.
and somehow does not seem saddened by this.

but i run this through my mind for weeks.

because even when i stare at a door
with the knowledge that it should remain closed.
with the knowledge that it most likely closed for a
    reason.
even then, i am trying to work out the best way to
    pick the lock.

everything ends. everything ends. everything ends.

but my heart still whispers, *does it have to?*

unwanted

in my dreams, i do not search for you.

i see you and light a match.
i see you and put my finger on the trigger.
i see you and run a marathon and write three books
and tell you how i have been better off without you
and i mean it.

i see you and do not note the way time has aged you.
i see you and do not wear grief.
i see you and hang grief in the closet
on an old wire hanger.

untouched, unneeded, unwanted.

i see you and do not stay in the closet.
do not think about the leaving.

do not think that maybe i am
the untouched, the unneeded,

the only unwanted thing in the room.

the day is ready for you

redlined

fact: we remember what we wish to.
the rest gets redlined, clean slated, washed and
neatly folded in the bottom of the sock drawer.

fact: i never said i needed you.
i only ever call because i am lonely.
or it is cold out. or i am lonely.

fact: nothing about you stuck.

fact: even if i remembered how forest fire bright
your eyes are, how flickering and wild,
(which i don't)
i would not write about you.

fact: see, i write only about important things.
the kind that make your chest ache,
or your knees rattle. so,

fact: this is really more about me
and how i am forgetting you slowly
and how frustrating it is that
the sun is high and i miss you.

fact: i still haven't made any space for you in the dresser.
the memories are all stacked on the bed. piles and piles.
and i will get to them soon. someday soon. really soon.

fact: usually, i am up well past midnight
folding and unfolding.
trying to get the corners right.
trying to figure out

the best place to keep you hidden.

nerves

my lungs cage restless moths,
frail little creatures.
too big and yet too fragile
to be moved.
too wild to be plucked out by the wing.

they are 3 AM dancing.
and somehow i am shoes in hand and anxious,
the only one with a curfew.

all i have is earthquake breath,
it rattles the doors like knees without bone.

and i have become terrified to say anything
that might pick the locks.

the day is ready for you

<u>wanting</u>

the sky in its dark, brooding midnight black
stretches out before us like a spool of twine
unwinding around the stars.

and when the day is quiet, when we think no one is
    looking,
we reach up our arms like maybe
we can grasp just a strand or two,
like maybe we, too, can be something bigger.

what is it about humans that always leaves us wanting?

we wonder what it's like up there in the clouds, in the
    endlessness.
if being so high up makes breathing easier or harder.
if we will ever find out what it's like to fly and if we
    do,
will we spin around and around the moon like giddy
    kids
or will we hover and contemplate what we left behind.

but then we find some other thing
to grab our attention.
we are such flighty birds, such utter romantics.
we will kiss each other on open mouths
and breathe promises into existence
and when we fall asleep,
we will both dream about
the white feathered backs of wings.

temporary

gravity never quite drew blood from us.
we spin, dizzy.
we keep our feet running.
not away, only forward,
they say we are only dreamers,
but in dreams
we become something more, don't we?

we joke that we are limitless
but we mean it.
we have decided on freedom.

and so it isn't that we know nothing of staying
it is just that we believe in casting
a wide enough net to touch
everything even if
only temporary.

the day is ready for you

picket fences never mattered, not to me

your breath,
mimicking my
own,
is an orchestra of
plump fruit.
pears. peaches.
something juicy and running.
warm bread rising
somewhere.
the blessing of being.

i don't need to tell you
that the ceiling leaks.
the floors have been gutted
and cold mornings make
frost dance on every glass surface.

but honey,
the raven still sings outside
our crooked fence,
and autumn sighs with it.

so i strum the soft skin
of your chest and
know it is my chest, too.

like glass

how prettily everything
(everyone)
seems to flutter around
her delicate features.

and i wonder,

what it would be like
to not be so ice
and blunt and brutal?

maybe i would float
like glass after an explosion.

maybe i would be soda pop and love letters
or sticky-sweet like syrup
oozing from the bottle.

maybe i don't really care to be all light.

what if i put boulders under my tongue
and in my pockets on purpose?

maybe i do.
maybe

i don't care at all.

the day is ready for you

playing cards

it is okay not to know,
or to know and be okay
with inconsistencies.

there will always be those
who trust and those who question.

but

some things are meant to be stories.

some pages are ripped out
and lit
because they tell the truth.

this is learning which
kind of faith
you hold.

do you need to know?

do you need to hold facts
between your fingers
like playing cards?

or does the knowing
undo the believing?

gain or lose

there is sweat on the neck of his shirt.
the sun is not high today,
which means he is nervous. he should be.

he smells like the inside of a car
that does not belong to him.
the kind that keeps perfume
and chewing gum in the glove box.

he hands me sunflowers and soft handfuls of poetry
but there is still dirt under his nails.

as if he bent down in my front yard, my own little
    garden,
the one i tend and water.
stole only words he thought i would not miss,
but i spend my days observing the almost invisible
    details.

i miss nothing.

now the petals will curl with age.
the metaphors will peel back one by one
until they all sound more like apologies.

he looks at me as if i should be grateful.
i see only things that once
belonged to me presented as a gift.

and i think, does this mean
i have gained something or lost something?

i cannot be sure.

the day is ready for you

forging

we forge whole worlds in the pits of our stomachs.
nestle vines between our palms.
urge them to bloom but only if they do so discreetly.

we live stories. live wars. live wars that become stories.
become indispensable in our homes.

(yet always feel dispensable.)

and i want more for my daughter.
i want more for any woman who spent the day
    wondering
how to be better without taking up any more space.

wondering how to become permanent fixture.

wondering why no one listens to her flower tongue
unless the words sound sweet.
meaning, why no one takes her seriously.

wondering how to breathe softer.
make less noise. make more money.
make someone else happy. accept defeat when asked to.
do, bend, break. *because she is woman.*

we create from nothing. we are sisters, mothers, friends.
    all.

and yet, still. still.

we spend lifetimes trying to undo our own spines.

uncertainty

mumbling over
my own tongue,
so fat and full.

like grapes
never plucked
from the vine.

my tongue is
alcohol spilling;
time drunk and burdensome.

every word tastes like uncertainty.
like tar black midnight
in the quiet of the afternoon.

truthfully, i just want to say
i love you and
have that be enough.

the day is ready for you

insistent

i have known this heart
to be brutal in nature.
frenzied as a starved beast
at the first sight of love.

somehow i am always, at once,
standing on solid ground
and
teetering on the edge
of this insistent
heartache.

if i love you it is not because
you have always been
irreversibly mine,

it is because you
have always been
irreversibly drawn to
light
in a way i do not
understand.

sometimes

growing attached to / all of the soft / that hangs
off your shoulders / a freshly washed sweater

we are coming undone / and it is
for good reason / sometimes / i wash my coffee
down with what we used to be / even before
the tender of you / forgot what it is to be tender

tumble dry / low heat

the shoulders hang wrong / tug off skin / soft but
not in the way warmth should be

there is a small stain in the
left-hand corner / red wine / or blood / something
unchangeable in the fibers / it is having a hard time
letting go / and i think / it looks a lot like us

the day is ready for you

love letter
---

this is a letter i will never send.
or a letter i will put in your mailbox
every morning until you read it.
(i haven't decided.)

a thank-you card that does not express gratitude.
a love note without any feeling in the pages.

maybe it should be an apology.
as long and sprawled out as a novel.
written only in ornate declarations.

but it isn't.

no, this is a letter just to say,
like something stuffed into a jar,

there was never enough air for me here.

learn

the garden is all stars tonight
and each one is named
after a woman who walked away.

i hope i learn from them.

the day is ready for you

moment

it is not enough
if when love comes
i am able to keep it
only for a moment.

my heart is too loud,
too demanding,
for love
to greet me at the door
and then disappear
as if it were never
really there.

only a guest
that did not make
reservations, after all.

<u>unsteady</u>

out of these hollow parts,
that voice dredges up the birth
of something like a dozen monsters.

the sound is unsteady.
or i am unsteady in its presence.

like i am the edge of a moving ship
or an amusement park ride
that should have stopped but hasn't.

and when it ceases,
i have to admit that it is partially my
tight grip on the railing
that leaves the bruises on my palms.

i spend most nights arms open.
i spend most nights fingers curled,
but empty as the whirling wind of a drum.
empty as the glass with the bottom cracked.

empty as the vowels
in the back of your throat.
churning, churning.

in the end, i would not know
what to do with full hands.

the day is ready for you

one after the other

here, this is for you:
the story of rage stolen from
the center of a storm.
gifted to a human.

have you heard this one?
heard of the hands wringing
themselves dry in stairwells,
snapping joints one after the other.

heard of the pacing. the hunting. the desperation.
the anger that left everything red or red turned ash.

heard of the candle burned down to the wick.
(what we do for such
little measures of peace.)

heard of the greed. the rampant jealousy.
the fruit we ate and hoarded.

even now.
years and years and wars
and wars and

no one has managed
to give it back.

mistaken

you, a car crash.
me, a blade mistaken
for a flashlight in the dark.

i think you have mistaken me
for a flashlight in the dark.
i think we have, on our worst days,
wounded each other.
on our best days,
spent too much time searching.

the day is ready for you

the best kind

we are the worst kind of strange.

the prowling ghosts that cling to the edge
of rooms they are not sure
they should be in.
the kind of kids that
think of fireplaces
yawning open before breakfast.
but we don't mind.

we hold hands with each other
on the playground
or behind the bleachers.

(let everyone believe
what they want to believe.)

but when we lie out on
your trampoline past midnight,
we always say the same things.

no one knows
dreams like we do,
do they?

you make this day
feel like dreams
met with open arms.

a restless
pause

the day is ready for you

<u>walk</u>

we bloom and it is harmless.

or sometime after midnight
we unfold our wounds like silk sheets.

or the night refuses to let go of us.
or we refuse to let go of the night.

or we make temporary homes out of each other.
this is how artists break their own hearts.

or something about your skin feels familiar.
like a memory, like a window
in a building i've stood in before.

or we teach each other a new language after all.

or this?

this is how we learn to walk again.

mine

everything is waterlogged.
we meant to jump ship. we did. really.
but i bite my knuckles and
you never stop me from second-guessing.

some people just don't know their way
around storm clouds, do they?

then it was splinters and screaming and wet.
ocean and new and foreign land.

we make our homes where we can. we have to.
no one teaches love before survival anymore.

secret: mine has always been in you.

so when i pick your weeds out of the concrete
and pretend they are wildflowers,
i mean to say that even in this wreckage

you are wanted.

the day is ready for you

language

we communicate
with hands and eyes.
it is our accidental language.
we learned it clumsily,

but i think we will keep it.

empty space

you told me you can either be bitten
or swallowed by love.

but i had already tucked away my heart
like loose strands of hair behind cold ears.

i was already open mouthed and screaming.

you said, *let it go.* you said, when you hold air
in your lungs like a crawl space in the attic,
soon enough it is bound to be
more kidnapping than inhale.

but a shovel makes the same sound
burying you alive as it does setting you free, does it
    not?

maybe i was just making a bad habit
out of romanticizing pain.
sometimes love ends. i suppose it did not have to
    stay.
owed me nothing. had no prior obligations here.

you said, *let it go.* and i have tried.
but even with all the blood,

why would i want to go from
holding the weapon to clutching empty space?

the day is ready for you

nothing

the leash has
never been necessary.
not for anything,
he said.

you cannot will it
into existence.

you cannot force
it into permanence.

come here.
crack open my bones.
i need you to understand
that nothing
stays forever.

not me.
not this.

not
even
love.

we are and we are not

but everything is solid around the edges.
the wind blurs the lines only for a little while.

it is still real, tangible.

like the grass or the mountains that run on and on,
they are. they just are not everywhere.

an explanation:
if we are holding hands one day but not the next,
it does not mean we are not still lovers.

we are only not making love at this moment.

i am trying to come to terms with this.
wanting does not always mean
i haven't found what i am looking for.

so when it rains, gold and glittering,
hollowing out the streets
and making new rivers in the pavement,

you are across town and i am in the living room.
we are and we are not together.

all at once.

the day is ready for you

<u>poetry</u>

you can
write the words.

but this
unfolding

(this becoming)

does not
always
mean
there will be
poetry.

intentions

we deserve some measure of softness. even when we
  don't.

knowledge

when they tell you of your frailty,
of your delicate nature.
when they remind you of the limitations
to your femininity, to your voice, to your body.
when they compare you. as if you should be
a lighter, darker, thicker, smaller
version of skin. of muscle. of bone.
as if the soul holds no relevance.

when they tug your ear.
when they begin the *sh sh* of whispers.

pour like an indoor rain.
pour like the earth should start again.
like a storm without pause.
like a whirling metaphor of sharp claws
and sharper words.

perhaps, if we are descended
from the rib cage of man,
man should learn how
to take care of his own body.

show them what it looks like
to be powerful. *to know it.*

my own way

you crack that grin without pause,
cheeks peach nectar blush
as you throw back your head.

how the heat runs
feverishly down your neck.

how i want to be touching you
until i am also a flower
or something else as sweet and open.

and i'll say it again. and, again, i'll say it.
i'll say it again and again.

the poem and i are tongue-tied.
the poem and i bitter argue
about which metaphor to use.
(i always come away sore and defeated.)
the poem and i know that without you
the words do not make sense.

listen closely.
when i am touching you, i am writing.
and when i am writing, in my own way,
i am touching you.

the day is ready for you

oh, i am

except sometimes i battle the idea of wholeness,
and why i cannot find it in the small of his back,
or with his hands cupped around my thighs
like undiscovered rivers.

because he is nothing if not running water,
while i boil and boil.
i sit on the counter simmering for days
until i am bone-dry.
until it is only glass and thirst.
(anger is a jealous master.)

the truth and the lie:
i am full. but i do not know the source.
i am full. but i have not yet poured from my own
     reserves.
i am full. but i do not know if i am whole.

(are these one and the same?
am i balancing words on my tongue
that do not have the same meaning?)

i breathe and honestly;
all the crisp air. all the morning shadows.
all the birds that sing outside my window.

(his hands his hands his hands)

oh, i am full.

limitations

everything begins before you tell it to.

the day is ready for you

the living

we don't smoke cigarettes anymore.
i stopped when we met.
when you discovered me like an answered prayer.
one i had been palms together and knees bruised for.

i could never tell if it was yours or mine
but i am not sure it ever really mattered.

we were both doing fine before.
if fine is a concise way of saying
we were dying just as slowly as everyone else.

getting by on the kind of love that disappears by
    dawn.
and we did get by. just not in the way we wanted to.

we had not yet decided to stay here.
hadn't made up our minds about living yet.

hadn't decided if the sweat and tears
and breathing and breathing and breathing
made us desire more or less.

but now? now, all i think about is your heartbeat.
and your ten-miles-per-hour laugh.

and your mouth. how it opens on mine like
    something blooming.

how i so very much like being alive.
and how it is nice. the staying. the living. the loving.

<u>here</u>

in between smacks of thunder,
we pull ourselves up by the teeth
and kiss the sky.
we listen to no one.

we belong here.

the day is ready for you

desire

there is something sticky-sweet about loving
and not needing to announce it.

you always violin your fingers
across my thigh in the car.
even when the leather seats are hot
and the air is humid heavy.

you smile that half-silly half-wicked grin.
it is kind of like a vow, kind of like
an unsaid, starry-eyed promise.

we never needed black ink
or courthouse letters.

we have something like forever.

what else could anyone possibly desire?

ghost town

you must have been waiting there.
you must have turned the porch light on.
you must have been waiting there
with the porch light on all night.

maybe i got there right after the fuse blew.
and you, all anger and impatience,
cursed the electric company,
went down to the basement,
couldn't figure out the wires.

(you always did have trouble with those.)

so maybe you ran out to the store
and and and
your phone died.
you couldn't find a pen
to leave a note in the dark.

maybe i got there right after you
hurried out of the driveway.

and maybe that is why it
looked like such a ghost town.

maybe that is why
it seemed to be so dark, so quiet.

maybe that is why
i was greeted by nothing
but moon and
a whole house that
did not answer
when i called your name.

the day is ready for you

<u>missing or loving</u>

i will love you until
loving you becomes a memory.
becomes a consequence.
until loving you looks more like
the exit sign of a local pub
and a lot less like your eyes.
until it sounds like talking back to old voice mails
and not like your laughter at all.

i will hold my own hand.
brush my thumb along my knuckles.
tell myself i find comfort in my own cold skin.
i will ask strangers on the street if they
have ever known happiness and
they will all stare at me blankly or
yell about my liquor breath.
but i think i did once. with you.
it wasn't like i had imagined.
it was more straightforward
and less break into song.
it was simple.
but the way i remember it,
i think i did.

but now?

now, i forget the difference
between missing and loving.

maybe there isn't one.

hear me out

we are finding new ways to rearrange our pieces.
you, rows and rows.
me, shoved beneath the bed or untouched.
truthfully it's hard to remember when this life
became less high school and more jigsaw.

the world, with its loud microphone and shut tight
    ears,
keeps saying that nothing is broken.
but how can that be if the only way to let the light in
is to crack the walls a little more?

yes, i know we are only getting by to get by now.
we have been for a while.
we do nothing but attempt to survive
and somehow call that living.

but look, hear me out.
my fingers have been crossed
behind my back for years.

i haven't promised anyone anything, see?

i've still got time.

the day is ready for you

pressure

the gravity of loving you.

(is a tidal wave. a crime scene.
an inhale. a pressure point.)

solid

in fact, it happened right here.
you told me we were skipping town.
yelled out the window of your car,
we are about to bear witness to a miracle.

and we did. the stars, the height, the spinning orbits.
the night unfolding around us like papier-mâché
    houses.

i hoped we would remember this as something
more solid than a dream or
way to pass the sticky months of summer.

we pressed closer, our mouths kiss-drunk swollen.
breathless and heated, each corner tucked into
    another.

it was unclear what belonged to me and what didn't.

you laughed about the magnitude of being this small
in the middle of something so much more infinite.
i laughed, too. i tried. the noise was more strangled,
like i was trying to find humor in my own funeral.

the truth or the secret was (is) that i love(d) you
like an endless seattle rain.
and i was daily certain that
was the only kind of infinity that mattered.

the day is ready for you

too little

concept: we color each other
with graceful precision.
you wear lilac and i will
wear chartreuse like a
dripping badge of honor.

let's leave stains on the carpet,
and remember that, even
slathered in brushstrokes,
in heavy and too little,
we are immaculate.

even if we exist as
nothing more today than
two bursting hearts
connected by painted limbs.

we are as open as the sky.
as swirling and dark and brilliant.
we can go on living despite it all.

just look at how vibrantly
we have breathed today,
in this one afternoon.

imagine a lifetime.

faith

but sometimes the only thing you can do
is hold on with your little, stubborn heart and have
    faith.

the day is ready for you

weapons

strange. how the weapons did not wound us.
the battle-axes, the knives, the sharp, sharp words.

how the enemy climbed over our garden walls
and into our towns. crept through our windows,
jazz music slow. pressed pointed edges against our
    skin.
spit around their own tongues,

you will never be enough.

what could we do but accept defeat?
wish for no more bloodshed? but no. no, we

tell them that *they are not real.* laugh in their faces.
tell them that this? this is all just one big metaphor
for how there will be people who wish to tear you
    down.
people who will grab and claw and strike by any
    means necessary.
that it will feel like war. that it will feel like all you
    have is enemies.

but no. no, we have decided not to give them any
    power.
and that means that this is a one-sided discussion.
a one-sided battle. a nonexistent power struggle.
and so we laugh. we belly laugh.
we see them through the curtains
and laugh until we are breathless.
we yell, *turn back now.*

because i promise, no one can gain ground here
if we keep our feet (our hearts) rooted. firmly.

caught

it is so messy lately,
and we are caught in the middle.
i've been thinking,
maybe we have to start at the beginning.

remind ourselves.
what did love look like
when it was still innocent?

i can hardly remember.

this partnership stretches around
us for miles, compatible and violent.

we have forgotten the art of
making love to each other.

we have forgotten what romance
tastes, sounds, feels like.

and i think, maybe, we should just start from scratch.
pause and rewind. begin before it all settled in,
like dust in unswept hallways.

hit play only after we figure out why
we slowly stopped
touching each other the way we used to.

and then, begin again.

the day is ready for you

stolen

we will not let the world steal us from ourselves.

fear

close your eyes.
let fear control nothing.

the day is ready for you

blindfolded

overthinking:

my feet run of their own volition.
they either slow gallop or pitter patter,
but they haven't learned how to stand still
long enough to grow roots. something about
   abandonment? not sure.

my arms hang at my sides, like useless windshield
   wipers. or paper fans.

i speak but it is a made-up language. no one
   understands the words.

my head blindfolds itself just so it can fumble
   anxiously in the dark.

i think a lot about your eyes, though. usually
   unwillingly.
and how painful it is to be in a room full of people
with such empty pockets, and words that are
so heavy i cannot lift them from the fog.

listen, nothing works when i tell it to.

but, oh, i wonder if your mouth still tastes anything
    like poison.
or if you've learned a new way of speaking in my
    absence.

or if i could only get the wheels to turn slower,
more efficiently, maybe we could try this
whole relationship thing one more time.

i don't know, honestly.

maybe if i think about it a little more.
yeah, i just need, like, a day or two.

maybe i'll just think about it, okay?

the day is ready for you

something like

being close to you
is something
like
blood underneath
fingernails.

meaning,
we have been
both
prey and predator
and somehow
we are
still alive.

understanding

quiet as an inhale,
the moment stretches between us,
and it is a continent we will never cross.
we haven't learned anything.

we never picked up the art
of swimming or building bridges
or understanding body language.

so we do not cross water.
we do not cross land.
we do not interpret the silence.
we just let it grow.
and grow.
and grow.

there are miles
between this one
hesitation and my arms.

there are miles between us.

the day is ready for you

fingerprints

make a decision to make the most of your two
hands.

<u>morning</u>

you are
the greatest secret.

if i could, i would
hold you
between my hands
like morning.

or something
like a whisper.

or something like
lightning trapped
in a glass bottle.

in other words,
i want to be the one
to keep you.

the day is ready for you

storm

i am having a hard time
focusing on the edge of his voice.
it is a blunt, cutting thing.

i do my best not to let it wound.

still, all i want to do is bury myself
in the nape of his neck.

and when it storms,
i startle awake.

angered and
pressed up
against his chest.

if i stay any longer
i will have to admit,

i do not know
what i am doing here.

slow

forgiveness
is a slow trickle.
like a heartbeat,
like rain.

the day is ready for you

this way

in this way,
we too
know of agony.
the scratch of life
at the door
despite the hour.
the half smile
of impatience
as it runs
sharp nails
against the wood,
beckoning us into
some dimly lit place.
(though maybe
i keep my eyes closed.)
we try to exist here
with pressed-close bodies
and noise
but simply
do not know how.

questions for a lover

the truth is

i am hoping your hands
know a thing or two
about tenderness.

the day is ready for you

silver spoon

do you or do you not know
what it's like to become a blade
in a house made of cigarettes and glass?

do you have to leave
the lights on
even when your eyes are shut?
i have. i do.

i often wonder if i was born left-handed.
and instead of teaching me,
my body decided it would be better
if i spent ten years with bruised fingers.

that is to say, i know it's late.
and my phone calls are more spilled blood
and crooked teeth than reason, but i miss you.
i wrote you a letter but everything was spelled
    wrong.

the paper smelled like smoke.
like i had written it with my eyes closed,
with the lights off, with the wrong hand.
like an apology i cannot get right.

i know i am more sharp edge than girl lately.
but i am trying to be more left-handed.
more tentative. more blush.
more fragile. more silver spoon.
less butcher knife.

<u>unknown</u>

i wear rivers like scarves
in every season.

all tied up in a knot
or hanging loosely to my waist,
it doesn't matter.

i am never too hot or cold for
some kind of cleansing.

so i wonder

what little poems
you whisper
when it rains.

and if they are spoken
softly, softly.

if the rain makes music
from tiny prayers.

i wonder if you, too,
know that
love does not
need to be known
to be real.

the day is ready for you

seek them, too

and the small joys.
keep them.

these bones

tell me what it means to be human.

i can feel this
blood and these bones.
but i have yet to decipher
the fine print.

everyone keeps telling me
to use these hands
only for good.

to use my heart like a soaring wind.

to use my mind like a library or
an open-ended something.

and i think they mean to tell me
that i have a choice. that some people
do not do these things.

and maybe that is why
my voice always curls around me
like smoke,
like a question mark.

the day is ready for you

<u>out</u>

come out of the in-between.
something better is waiting.

prayers like
exhales

the day is ready for you

further

granted, we have been here before.
the place of teeming burdens.
the place of weary, weary bones.

(grief is heaviest when it runs rampant.)

but it never lasts forever, does it?
there will always be a little sun that shines
through makeshift curtains or
a little miracle tugging on the hem of something.

and then, when you have answered.
even if answered with snowstorm tongue.
even if citrus bitter and howling.
we can wrap around each other and
watch as the shadows all spill down your shoulders.
watch the billowing waves.
watch as they dissolve into nothing more
than distant worries.
(further and further)

further and further.
further and.
further.
and.

above all

i am learning to hold *i'm sorry*
between my teeth like a cherry stem
instead of a water fountain.

above all, deliberately.

the day is ready for you

told you

and when it stops. the love, i mean.
i am always there waiting.
i do not say *i told you so*. at least, not this time.
(the art of biting one's tongue and all)
but i do not rub your back, either.

because, one day, when love comes and stays.
(which it will. it will.)
when love is the kind of love
that you deserve.
when love understands your nervous laugh
and your fear of heights.
when love does not run away.
when love eats dinner with you on the floor.
and love lets you steal the blankets.
and love holds your hand no matter where you are.

on that day, i will tell you.
on that day, i will make sure you know.
you have always been worth loving.
remember?
i told you so.

i know
___

the thing about
softness is—
it already exists
within your chest.
i have heard your
butterfly wing
laughter,
i know.

the day is ready for you

drop them

but you can live without them, you know.
the devils. the demons. the unsaid things.
the heavy weights. the guilt.
the regret. the bitterness. the copper tongue bite.

the boys who did not know how to love you.
the years you did not know how to love yourself.

and the mistakes. the mistakes. oh, the mistakes.

the ones that make your chest tight.
the ones you try to wash clean.
the ones you've scrubbed and scrubbed
beneath moonlight and bedsheets and showerheads.

you can live without them, you know.

look, your sweaty hands.
look, your shaking bones.
pry your fingers off the triggers.
drop the guns.

bravery

a confession—
the answer is simple.

like the wind whistling
through everything,

take up as much
space as you dare.

the day is ready for you

<u>exhales</u>

from a distance,
everything pales and shrinks,
does it not?

even love. even the greatest love.
even grief. even loss.
even the backs of our eyelids
as we drift and drift and sleep.

think of the moon. how we must
appear so small. so fragile.
so insignificant.

but how up close

we are a whole universe
expanding
in tiny, tiny exhales.
truthfully

i will tell you again and again:
in some small way, everything matters.

open windows

forgive me for my daydreams. i am drifting
through the afternoon. lazily. dizzily.
my breathy laughter scatters fallen leaves
to the wind and this dictates nothing.

honey becomes clouds
in my tea or perhaps
lemons become lace around my thighs—
there is no telling.

i have spent over twenty years
with a full head of possibilities,

all married to each other in some untold way.

i only let the world
gaze through the window.

the poem is a window.

there will always be whispers as hammers.
hammers masked as whispers.

but i refuse to let the glass shatter.

the day is ready for you

fits

i carry memories as second skin.
i lace them up and around my limbs.

a thousand old sweaters that still smell of
   honeysuckle.

sunday, the image of my father's jaw as it cracks into
   a smile.

tuesday, the gap in an old lover's teeth.
the outline of his hair against the pillowcase.

thursday, all of my sister's smiles.
i let them become part of my smile, too.

friday, a mug of something hot and steaming.
the burning pressure against palms. the slow way it
   fades.

monday, only the sun. how it brings out your
   freckles.
how you curl your hair around your finger in the
   summer.

always, as the day ends, i am wearing some
kind of love from someone. someone who has loved
or still loves or may one day love me.

even as i sleep i am trying on new moments. it all
   fits.

name you

daughter,
i will name my heart
after you.
both having been born
in the body,
both being my
dug deep roots.
my grace givers.
oxygen providers.
safe keepers.

i would not exist without you.

and so i name it after all
that you are
and
will be,
little one.

i name it: resilient.
i name it: courageous.
i name it: fearless.

i name it: love.

the day is ready for you

keeping

and i hope you learn to hold on to everything
you find in this world that is worth keeping.

ask the wind

i dig my nails into the forest floor and pull up
    cobblestones.
there is no part of anything that has remained
    untouched.

wind swallows the trees, trees swallow the rain,
rain swallows the ponds and rivers. it is ongoing.

so if i were to lend you a listening ear,
know that i have heard it all.
if i were to let you hold me,
know i have been held by different arms.

and that is not to say that it will not be beautiful,
but it will not be the same. everything leaves a mark.

someone once told me, bluntly, that all love hurts.

i told them i knew firsthand. secondhand.
i have heard it all before. and that is how i know.

anything that scars, heals.

and maybe, just maybe, is better for it.
ask the wind. ask the trees. ask the rivers.

the day is ready for you

honeyed

still
we worship that
temporary,
honeyed stillness
of the morning.

the crack of an eye
fluttering open like
thunder.
only softer,
softer.

to wake up next to
a lover and know them.

as if they have always been.
as if they always will be.

still
your hands
around my shoulders.

nothing has ever
come close to this.

only
---

i was so good at water under the bridge.
but with no bridge. only drought. only desert.

that is to say, no one else noticed
because i wore invisible over everything.

i found comfort in the smallest homes.
not studio-apartment-in-manhattan small.
more closet. more storage under the staircase.
(hunched shoulders, lowered eyes. quiet, quiet, quiet.)

even when it did not rain,
i carried an umbrella tucked under my elbow.
just in case.
all things not planned and checked
made my stomach drop.
all things loud drew too much attention.
what would they think? what would they say?
but there was no joy to be found in the shadows.
no joy hushed and whispered in the corner of some
   silent place.
listen: it does no good to hold caution
so tightly that no one is breathing.

so, five years later, i leap off of buildings in my spare
   time.
meaning, i am no longer afraid of change.
meaning, i shrugged off the fear like an unnecessary
   overcoat.
meaning, i threw caution to the wind and it did not
   come back.

and that is perfect. i do not want it.

the day is ready for you

so very

someday, the world
will try to wound you.
(will wound you)

all the same,
stay soft. stay kind.
stay so very tender.

worth

what witchcraft it is
that the sun
rises every morning
and does not ask
if it is time,
or if the sky is ready,
or if she has permission
to burn and
burn wildly.

what a treacherous thing,
this knowing
your power.
this recognizing
your worth.

the day is ready for you

unlearning

then, i opened my mouth to speak
and laughter roared.

(what malicious notes)

and i, no laughter remaining in my bones, became
    mouse.

first, observing from the corners,
hunger churning my stomach into campfire.

but then, aftcr, when the laughter did not cease,
i became human statue.

more silent than the sun. more silent than the slow
way it gnaws at your skin. vicious and burning.

i was learning the art of unlearning my own name.

now, i bite the neck of anyone who thinks
    themselves a god.
blood or no blood. i sink teeth into the skin. ask no
    questions.

once, i loved a man who told me i would never
    satisfy him.

then, i apologized. meant it. said i would try harder.
said don't let the laughter fool you, i can do better.
said i promised.

now, what i would give to bite him, too.

before the bridge

every year we grow and dwell
in different veins of the city.

i take the 1 train
as far down as it will go
before the bridge.

you walk everywhere.

we do not meet.

not on the corner of 18th and 7th,
or
when the train rumbles,
or
when it pours and the streets run
wet and muddy.

not when the sky caves in.
not when i use my own two feet.

(or the train is delayed.)

still, i would walk for you.

anywhere. everywhere.

the day is ready for you

is it the growing up

concept: the sun sets and the sky looks like raspberries.
we reach up and take one from a bush, bursting and
    juicy.
the clouds touch our fingers shyly and we
laugh and laugh until our stomachs hurt in the best
    way.

concept: we are becoming dull with age.
i tell you about the raspberries and you tell me
we are too old to believe in magic.
i ask, *is it the growing up that leaves us empty?*
you stay silent.
the next morning there is
a note on the counter.
fear, it says. *fear*.
i wonder how much courage
it took to write it down.

concept: a home in which fear is an invite-only guest.
and we do not send an invitation. do not even throw a
    party.

concept: the day ends and you barge into our bedroom.
yell and yell. grab my arm. chase me out into the night.
you say, *look at the sky*. it is all cranberry and red.
look, see how the wind grows strawberries?
see the fields? how they breathe on indefinitely?
and, lord, the look on your face. it is breathtaking.
your mouth twisting up in joy.

concept: we eat from the vine.
the stars wink their little eyes at us.
the moon listens as we weave her a story.
nothing stills until dawn.

concept: we stay here forever.
fear does not reach us in this place.
it is only our front yard but it is wild.
it is brimful with dreams.
it is an accomplishment. to grow and still believe.

it is magic. it is ours. in the best way, it is ours.

the day is ready for you

<u>processing</u>

all of us,
despite our hearts

(and their violent
tendencies)

are in the process
of surviving.

everything

you are. an autumn sunrise. a cloud. a storm.
spring. warm rain. a flood. a whisper. a surprise
     party.
a verse. a flickering light. march. april. may.
an argument. laughter. drying ink. old love.
the sweetest friendship. a bright morning.
a new day. hands. breath. cold. falling snow.
an open mouth. december. january. february.
home. skin on skin. crooked teeth and smiles.
a song about loneliness. a song about triumph.

you are. a full-belly meal. september. october.
     november.
a movie theater with cupholders. a slow evening.
something soft. feathers. fresh mango.
vintage sweaters. black-and-white photographs.
whispers. calligraphy. hot sand between toes.

you are breakfast in bed.
june. july. august. stained-glass windows.
an old building. evergreens. an endless metaphor.
an ocean. every ocean. everything.

the day is ready for you

but it is worth it
_____

when was the last time
i was barefaced and brave.

let my freckles line
my cheeks like
miniature tin soldiers.

did not come undone
by the soft circles
under my eyes,
each the color of plums
or deep bruises.

or woke and commanded
the day to rise with me.

i cannot explain it
but if i were a poem,
i do not think i would
have written myself yet.

this learning to
love myself
is taking so much
time.

most

perhaps, we are most courageous when we let go.

the day is ready for you

all at once

look at this day,
so vast and sweeping.

i have spent the better half of
the afternoon trying to be
everywhere all at once.

now, let me greet the sky.
open my arms to
all of this unruly air.
feel the grass
between my toes.

i want to know
that there are
good things coming.

because there are.

there are
good things
coming.

tell everyone

the greatest secret:
learning to keep your heart
wildly, wildly open.

the day is ready for you

someday

someday
they will name streets
after us in every
suburban neighborhood.
people will know about our love
as normal
dinner table
conversation.
it will be a bedtime story,
campfire tale.
they will whisper
to each other
on buses and planes.
in offices, at bars,
in hotel rooms,
on first dates.

they will say
we were the ones
who made it.

see, did i not tell you:

in some way,
we will always linger.

unmistakably

idea: the cage door is only an illusion.
iron bars made of rusted fears.
we are unmistakably free.

idea: touch me like it's saturday.
remember what love looked like before padlocks.

idea: maybe if we admit to our uncertainty.
let go of our secrets like fireflies
we had no intention of keeping,
the world will taste sweeter.

idea: we are the color of sunrise. amber and rose.
no imagined shackles keep the sun from rising.
so why should anything keep you?

the day is ready for you

let it
___

come here. i need
to tell you a secret.

there is light waiting
to pour in through
the doorway.

let it.

let it flood.

happiness
---

with something
like happiness, they say,
you will need somewhere to hold it.

like a heart.
(yours or someone else's.)
like a hand.
(attached to a trustworthy body.)
like a dream.
(that does not know the definition of
unraveling.)
like faith.
(not moving. just listening.)

and i tell myself.
though i am not as old
or wise or educated,

that i should carry
my happiness in this once
empty space
between my shoulder blades.

like passion. like love.
like something so tangible
i can almost feel
its hot, hot breath.

the day is ready for you

<u>always</u>

oh, but to be felt in the bones.
remembered.

all sorts of things

like an ocean rippling through the night,
we sneak from windows.

but only when the sky looks like it
should be lace instead of storm.

there isn't light but
no one minds.
we do not need to see
to know;
we have each stolen things
with our eyes closed.

little moments. little stories.
a peck on the cheek.
the last seat on the bus.
a heart. (an accident.)
a chocolate bar. (on purpose.)

two different lovers. the taste of winter.

the time to do nothing but tell each other
    everything.
oh, we will steal that again tomorrow.
oh, we would steal all sorts of things if
the world would only let us.

the day is ready for you

what we have searched for vs. what we have found

the lost things.

bees. forests. sweat. parking lots.
august. socks in the dryer.
youth. change. resentment. every world but ours.
fear. old wounds. porcelain dolls.
the trampoline. hers and mine. schoolwork. essays.
snow. the kind you sink your teeth into.
loneliness. blue eyes. cigarette smoke.
long nails. fragile hearts. open knees.

the found things.

love.

commitment

the rain and i fell in love slowly.
it is hard to commit
to something that cannot stay.
only comes when the conditions are just so.
only comes when the ground needs it.
or the sky requires it.
or the day has been so dark
it comes almost out of spite.

it is unrequited but tender.
it leaves me almost
unrecognizable.
like an open floodgate.

even if sopping. even if a little ruined.

perhaps, that is how
i will love you, too.
with my face pressed against the glass.
until given the chance.
until everything is just so.

it is not a heavy weight

my hands are still nothing if not bone.
little lilies planted in the pavement of the city.
heavy velvet. sea-tossed air. breath that does not
    stain.
my grandmother's garden. garlic in her greenhouse.
raspberries in her wild forest. land that could only
    be magic.
her hands. all bone and skin and wishes, too.

oh, my friends. within my heart.
such women of joy. their weight is the weight i carry.
i carry it out of love.

my feet are nothing if not bone. foreign stones.
the outskirts of town. lovely yawning mouths.
taller trees. spinning. spinning.

and if i know anything, i know
blood does not make anything but war.
i waited all this time. but

at last. i know a little.
a little, at last.

alison malee

when

and when they
turn up their noses,
ask what
we are *still* doing here,
we will tell them
something about
being alive,
something about wanting
nothing more
than air in our lungs
and someone's
sweaty hand tangled in ours.

that for once
this living
and this breathing
and this smiling
and this existing
feel right
and are enough.

the day is ready for you

head down

i stretched myself thin, and i worked in the shadows.

always with my head down, always with my spine
 curved in.

and i didn't always know quiet. sometimes i had to
 gather
the courage to remain so, to not let anger or
 frustration
pull me from myself.

often, i approached myself like a stranger.

i tried to hold my own hand. whisper in my own ear.

tell myself that this is only temporary;
this overwhelming sorrow that seemed so paralyzing.

but even the *inhale exhale* of breath became poisonous
after too much time alone.

so i started spending afternoons in a garden.
found myself a little safe space.

started digging my hands in the ground.
let my fingers feel what it is like to become one with
    something.

at first, my belief was that if i spent enough time
bringing life into the world, i would also grow full.

i would feel the buds of new flowers bursting in my
    chest.
the opening of petals, the vibrancy of newly
    discovered beauty.
the crisscross of vines in my veins.

my hope was that the smell of the earth would lull
    me
into believing that i, too, was beginning.

the day is ready for you

<u>beginning</u>

grace is in the practice.
the red, brown leaves
falling at the end
of autumn.
the snow beginning
each winter.
the slow pressure
as you run your fingers
up my spine at dawn.
the way steam rises
from the bathwater
when it runs hot.
the sun encompassing the day.
the things that begin
over and over.
the redoing of it all,
even though
it is already
beautiful.
even though it
is already
just as it should be.
just for practice.

just because.

kind

wherever you are,
i hope the day
has been kind to you.

and at the very least,
held your hand.
and at the very least,
let you speak
only good things
into existence.

the day is ready for you

my only guide

something about the quiet.
i want to hold it close,
eat it up like a wide,
open landscape
in one inhale.

let it sit on the width of my tongue.
let it rush over me blindly.

wear it around my wrists.
not as an ornament
but as a reminder.

use only words as decoration
and silence as some other thing completely.

words as an entity i haven't met yet.
words as a vow. words as a promise.
words as a means to an end but also the end.
words as a disease.
the dawn and all its solitude as the cure.

let the quiet be my only guide.
let the quiet be my only guest.
let the quiet be the only thing that haunts me.
let the quiet be the only breath
i take that leaves me full.

hidden

the next tide came and
washed us out of its hair,
until the ground was velvet soft.

until the day no longer looked like
a prison sentence but a promise.

we only breathe freely with
our legs tucked into the ocean's current.

we try to be here as much as we can.

so when i tell you there is life
hidden in the floorboards.
or a plane ride. or a smile.
or the palm of a sweaty hand.
or saltwater tides.

listen closely.

the world can pause only for a little while.

what more will it take
for you to use
this heart in your chest
as a second chance?

the day is ready for you

note:

you do not have to
unravel gracefully.

yet

today i am going to move
and leave nothing behind.
which is to say, i am going
to unwind like porcelain stars.
which is to say, i will be my own miracle.
which is to say, this day will be endless.
which is to say, i have given up
on black and white.

i hold out my arms only for strangers
who look me in the eyes.
who notice nothing but the amber dust
of sunsets in my lashes.
(or) the gold reflection of many untold secrets.
(or) my incessant need for open skies.

which is to say, today i will be a river.
forward moving.

which is to say, i am a girl trying
to understand a map
without following directions.

i am not lost
yet.

the day is ready for you

remember
---

the trick is:
less comfort,
more courage.

epilogue

this is a prayer. a church taught quiet.

my mother taught folded hands.
my father taught question marks.

my friends taught luck of the draw.
except funerals. we all prayed at funerals.

my sisters and i do not know each other yet.

my grandmother taught faith.
my aunt taught self-reliance.

my husband taught trust in the unseen.
my mother-in-law taught the power of dreaming.

my children taught patience,
and in its own way, this is its own kind of prayer.

when i close my eyes, i taste constellations.
this is its own kind, too.

index

the day is
ready for you

Andrews McMeel Publishing
a division of Andrews McMeel Universal
1130 Walnut Street, Kansas City, Missouri 64106

www.andrewsmcmeel.com

18 19 20 21 22 BVG 10 9 8 7 6 5 4 3 2 1

ISBN: 978-1-4494-9298-4

Library of Congress Control Number: 2017952479

Editor: Patty Rice
Art Director: Diane Marsh
Production Editor: Elizabeth A. Garcia
Production Manager: Cliff Koehler

attention: schools and businesses

Andrews McMeel books are available at quantity discounts
with bulk purchase for educational, business, or sales
promotional use. For information, please e-mail the
Andrews McMeel Publishing Special Sales Department:
specialsales@amuniversal.com.